An Apology for Loving the Old Hymns

PRINCETON SERIES OF CONTEMPORARY POETS

OTHER BOOKS IN THE SERIES
Returning Your Call, by Leonard Nathan
Sadness And Happiness, by Robert Pinsky
Burn Down the Icons, by Grace Schulman
Reservations, by James Richardson
The Double Witness, by Ben Belitt
Night Talk and Other Poems, by Richard Pevear
Listeners at the Breathing Place, by Gary Miranda
The Power to Change Geography, by Diana Ó Hehir
An Explanation of America, by Robert Pinsky
Signs and Wonders, by Carl Dennis
Walking Four Ways in the Wind, by John Allman
Hybrids of Plants and of Ghosts, by Jorie Graham
Movable Islands, by Deborah Greger
Yellow Stars and Ice, by Susan Stewart
The Expectations of Light, by Pattiann Rogers
A Woman under the Surface, by Alicia Ostriker

JORDAN SMITH

An Apology for Loving the Old Hymns

Princeton University Press

Copyright © 1982 by Princeton University Press
Published by Princeton University Press, 41 William Street,
Princeton, New Jersey
In the United Kingdom: Princeton University Press, Guildford, Surrey

All Rights Reserved
Library of Congress Cataloging in Publication Data will be
found on the last printed page of this book

Publication of this book has been aided by a grant from
The Paul Mellon Fund of Princeton University Press

This book has been composed in Linotron Palatino
Design: Barbara Werden
Clothbound editions of Princeton University Press books
are printed on acid-free paper, and binding materials are
chosen for strength and durability

Printed in the United States of America by Princeton
University Press, Princeton, New Jersey

To Malie

*Such is the amount of this boasted immortality.
A mere temporary rumor, a local sound, like the tone of that bell
which has just tolled among these towers,
filling the ear for a moment—lingering
transiently in echo—and then passing away
like a thing that was not.*

Washington Irving, *The Sketch Book*

Contents

PART ONE
A Lesson from the Hudson River School

Constable Hall	3
Little Suite for Edvard Munch	5
Vine Valley	9
For the Orthodox	13
For Dulcimer & Doubled Voice	21
A Lesson from the Hudson River School: Glens Falls, New York, 1848	23
Sometime in the Twenties: A Photograph Never Found in the Mansion of a Man Dead by His Own Hand	31
A Side of Beef	33
Mount Hope: to Weldon Kees	35
A Lost Sonata	37
An Apology for Loving the Old Hymns	45

PART TWO
A Mirror for Loyalists

Walter Butler: Dispatches from the Mohawk Frontier, 1778	51
Guy Johnson: London, 1788	73
Joseph Brant: Niagara, 1804	81
Notes	89

Acknowledgments

Some of these poems have appeared, as follows:

The Agni Review
    Constable Hall
    The Vampire
    Vine Valley
    For the Orthodox (as Hymns: For the Orthodox)
    A Side of Beef
    Joseph Brant: Niagara, 1804 (as Niagara, 1804)
Epoch
    Self-Portrait with Burning Cigarette
The Georgia Review
    For Dulcimer & Doubled Voice
New England Review
    Guy Johnson: London, 1788 (as London, 1788). Reprinted by permission from *New England Review*, Vol. V, No. 1 (Autumn 1982). Copyright © 1982, by Jordan Smith.
The Ohio Review
    Self-Portrait with Wine Bottle
Pavement
    A Lesson from the Hudson River School: Glens Falls, New York, 1848
Shenandoah
    A Lost Sonata

PART ONE
A Lesson from the Hudson River School

Constable Hall

Constableville, New York

Here, simple description is not enough. These are cut stones rising
   through an August drizzle, gray gables, great cornices,
The roofline harsh against the sky, and the weathercocks rusting,
   swinging in a changing wind, the iron pickets darkening.
The door bolted, its paint etched away. And on the shutters, a pat-
   terned, elaborated journal of weathering . . .

But there is no one to read that script now. No one to bend the
   corner of a visiting card, and turn again toward the carriage
   drive,
Or to notice if the windows have taken on the steely air of rain in
   deep woods, if the brambles have moved closer.
Who will recall the small jets of the gas lamps; who will count the
   grain of oak stairsteps, the yellowed invitations on the mantel?

And how should I describe these rooms truthfully? You will not
   walk through them, nor will I. Or if we should, on a wet day, a
   day for failing sight,
Then we should see as I have always supposed spirits must, as if a
   great weight pressed against each eyelid, and the world had
   changed
To streaks of rain-water on an antique pane, something withheld in
   flaws and swirls of the glass, something given back:

A single lamp, perhaps, still burning in a room where so many
   years have been forgotten. But who could speak of that and be
   believed?

Little Suite for Edvard Munch

1. Self-Portrait with Wine Bottle

A father hides in the wine's dark, overripe
pit, in the bruise a bottle inherits
from the glassblower's cough. In this cafe,
the faces sag inward like spoiled grapes,

one bad seed rotting into another. Edvard,
you said disease, insanity, and death
hovered around your cradle. And all these words
ferment from one: Papa. Remember how

he held you, small as a fly, in his arms?
Neither do I. And still a father never
loses his grip. I taste him in the slow burn
of a bad year on my tongue, in the background

of lost faces where mine stands out, not lost,
not anything but a father's fist come home.

2. The Vampire

The title's wrong. You meant a kiss, just that.
And who hasn't been kissed this way: a lover's
lips bear down, take the world's full weight
and press it against your throat. The moon has risen

full and orange, and that dull light streaks
my wife's hair, streaks my neck. How many nights
I've buried myself in her arms, only to wake
so hungry to see my face rise in hers

that I call her by my own name as we kiss.
So this is what our loving comes to: our other life,
paired mirrors that go on forever past empty glass.
Edvard, you might as well have painted a moon

and the hollowness that eats it out. Lovers
closing, two crescents, two halves of nothing.

3. Self-Portrait with Burning Cigarette

Edvard, this could be your face or a match
flickering out, this little breath that barely
stirs the thick air. Some nights I sit alone
until my Lucky burns my hand, and watch

the smoke rise. Marsh gas in the fields,
or the stink of beached fish. Your rising sea,
the long grass gnawing at my barn stones,
whatever refuge we choose breaks apart like waves

into the trough, or hills in this upstate drizzle.
I spend the days with pliers and barbed wire
because the cries of children at play in my woods
leak through the walls into my sleep. Our faces

on canvas or a shaving mirror turn soft
as what our lives burn into: a blister, a fog.

Vine Valley

There will be nothing left to forgive. The inn
failing along the canalside, lattice-
work of beams and splintered panes. Beyond the lakes,
already there is the sound of windows breaking,
that vision of cold. So the landscape grows
deeper, a dryness in your throat
aging with the wine, marriage of spirit and bad weather.
On the hillside, two men with hooks work
toward each other along the vines. They've built a fire
by the road of leaves and blackened grapes,
and the porch shudders in the autumn sun.

This is what you meant by grief: a stroke of charcoal
lost against the dark weave of the scarf. That sorrow
is a spring seeping through matted leaves,
these roughened planks. The journal entries
thread their heavy weave around your throat,
and there is nothing left to say. Or only the white
script of fast water on the creek,
how her tears fell on the purple dress, darkening
rosary of amethyst and widowed fields. Early winter
reciting the year's last testament: the old man
is sick again, and the farm up for sale.

All you remember is the trellis of moonlight
over his face. He abandoned the fences
as the fields grew more difficult, empty as a house
without a single vase, or what a vase can hold:
Ash. The veins of each leaf
give up their vintage at last, simply and in flame.

You put your hand on my shoulder, and say it's past
time to thin the vineyard down. And we go out
where the firs reel like a farmer gone
half-blind from his glass of bad whiskey. If the shadow
of his hands tangled in your shadow as he fell,

if he only stood where the barn walls met, background
of shade and cracked siding, it was still the same: a fate
passed to us in the dim tracks cobwebs leave on stone,
gray weathered into a fainter gray. On the doorpost
you carved a tree nearly swallowed by vines
and two deer gnawing at the root. We called it home,
sweet interlacing of hunger and the world.
There was nowhere else to go. A house surrounded
by the fullness of grapes, of leaves turning the light
back from their stalks. Promise of early harvest
and a deed in your hand, settling all claims.

But out here the land is only a clearing, the sickle's
cry and passage. A failure of trust. The house
falls as if winter went on like a father
dying before your eyes, dying into himself, a brother
who won't step out of the shadows seen finally
for nothing but a slur of half-light interrupted
by the window slats. It would be so easy to let the snow
take everything now, take you, the way you wanted
even your elegy to blame itself for how you stood
between silver maples on the hillside, your arms
crossed with the white sun. I gave you up,

and there was no one left to speak. Once you wrote
all we are given are the steps of a mower
coming home in the evening along the sheaves.
The shaded lantern in a window marked with frost,
how it fell and shimmered as he passed between the trees.

That blame is a way of twisting another's death
into your own. So I confess I've taken you
into this field, as a foundling becomes half-kin.
You come toward me now down the rows of vines,
and we are so alike we must share even
this grief: that sorrow is original,

a fellowship of loss lying at the root of things.
You put the scythe in my hand, and we walk
where the smudge rises slowly from damped fires.
We will bury him together, before the early squalls,
while leaves still smoulder in the ditches. Because wine
tastes bitter without a trace of ash at its heart.
Because this is what brothers must do: forget,
as an empty house settles into its legacy of knotted stems.
As hearing the end of a father's story let us sleep, arm in arm,
at last, let even our sleep deepen into this curve
of night and the first snow, turning, gathering us in.

For the Orthodox

Marina Tsvetayeva, 1892-1941

A Moscow Invocation, 1916

Yes, I have called bereavement *most beautiful*
sister, she who requires my song, who insists
even if I am bashful and the few guests
bored. Why is she not welcomed in finer homes?
She is as kind as a gentleman's polished
mirror, white mistress of likenesses, as if
the heart were a field stiff with ice, as if
our griefs were the dire wolf who never feasts, who
lives only to scour these woods. As if the farms
blazed through snow, cold streets ran flaming with her voice.

An Open Letter to Emigré Friends in Paris, 1933

How I love the rich,
who even in their fall from grace
are never graceless. (The count who wipes the cafe floors
honors even me
with his smooth court bow, and I'm told
he overtips on his night off.) Yes, you would prefer
me bitter, I think,
but that is a tone too cheaply
acquired for my taste, and hard to lose. When I wrote how
my daughter blistered
her fingers in making bonnets
and five francs a day, which served just to preserve us
in our cold attic,

in our usual state of slow
starvation, your applause was like the cries of angels
who see the fine shirts
burning on the backs of the damned.
I want no more of it. And when I did not visit,
because my good shoes,
my only shoes, abandoned me
on the street outside your house, my apology read
like those bad novels
of Dostoevsky's, volumes stocked
with fools who believe their precious lodgings in heaven
are paid for in full
by the great sins of their neighbors
who owned, perhaps, an extra lamp or some china.
Let the covetous
have all they want, they still must live
in a world yawning with hunger. Let me remember
an old man who bows
because his pride requires it,
not the vanity of others. He owes us little else.

*To Her Husband, on His Disappearance into Russia,
   a Premonition, 1937*

Sergei, I cannot
   sleep. I must confess over
and over my one sin,
   that I always desired you
less than I craved knowledge
   of your forgiveness, my love,
our imperial road
   where we met like two strangers
who bow once and pass by.
   Oh, if we had joined hands there

and gone on together
  toward the rising mist, Japan,
some port where we'd forget
  how all things fail: grand hotels,
their caviar and cream
  dwindling at last to a thin
potato broth, bad wine,
  at a third-rate village inn . . .
I knew no other man
  who could forgive me the wise
clarity of my heart:
  I found I could love you more,
more, in your absences,
  and so I led my lovers
from my lips to my bed
  just so they too would leave
and my nights would wither
  except for this song, white priest
who blesses the marriage
  of our distant, strange voices
into one long lament.
  All the men I've loved are dead.
The sleek souls I gave them
  leave no more shade than bare trees.
But you, you are the light
  of winter, glare through branches,
ice in the sky, all these
  wonders that keep me awake.
Those songs I wrote were meant
  for those who shiver all night,
who cannot sleep, as you,
  poor man, could never find rest.
Those songs are dead. And I,
  I fear they will be your wreaths,
gifts of a wife who must
  always come too late. Sergei,

in my insomnia,
  I love you wholly . . .

On the Paris-Moscow Train, 1939

I think I always give myself to doomed things,
    which is the way of exiles,
  to love only what cannot be held:
    not streets, mountains, gilded spires,
but the heart, the domes and mountains of my heart!

Stone fathers of Germany, worn stones of Prague . .
    yes, all these will outlast me.
  Even the eagle, shorn of his wings,
    will be a gift to my son,
his icon: my body in its downward flight.

But I am the gift given all to myself,
    like steam off a last thick broth
  brewed for men who will give everything
    to join the white regiment:
mist, thin mist, settling on Moscow's hills.

To Her Daughter, from the Communal Kitchen of
    Yelabuga, 1940

And so my daughter
                we are reduced

to distant, bare rooms,
                these last scribbled

correspondences
                between unlike souls

who bear one name,
                one punishment.

Oh, when you forgot
all your dear poems
for a girl's duller
playthings, I knew
we would not be close
again. You were
so young to renounce
everything
I might have offered,
which was nothing
after all but words.
So few are left,
mostly your letters
where the censor
has never disguised
your long anger,
your longer desire
to be any
woman's child but mine.
I pity him,
poor bureaucrat, who
felt no duty
to destroy your lines
entirely, cold
lines he must have known
would sear my hands.
I pity myself,
who no longer
know the luxury
of guilt. Let me
tell you what I've learned
of poverty:
things are as they are.
I pity you,

all of us, condemned

                    to the extreme

penalty: to have

                    only coarsest

emotions left. Don't

                    share your sorrow,

tell me how things are.

                    Tell me truly,

do they allow you

                    a rope to hang

your clothes? I have one

                    before me now,

my loyal, frayed god

                    who says perhaps

there may be an end

                    to this dying,

a day when fires blaze

                    again, and pain

goes to ground. Perhaps

                    Alya even

we may join hands then.

Before Her Suicide, Yelabuga, 1941

1. I Have Heard the Wind

Yes, I have heard the wind call me bitter
even in spring, and have seen my name scrawled
in vacant margins of a long, gray sky.
And those sharp sprigs of the new wheat,
do you think I do not know at whom their fingers point?

Do you think I do not know who I am?
That is one lesson the world teaches,
a harsh, difficult language learned by rote . . .
Listen, there is a flight of jays,
their harsh cry. Do you think I do not know my voice?

There is a taste of dark tea, overbrewed,
the burnt crust of my tongue. There is a prayer
prayed in bitterness for those who vanish.
I have heard the wind fall silent.
Do you think I do not know a blessing when it comes?

2. For the Orthodox

Grandfather, I thought of you at prayer even
as I prayed because I could not love a god
who did not have your face. I think if I lived
again I would be just a man who harvests
his own wheat, whose sabbaths are given to Christ,
who believes those torn, tender features are more
than a mere likeness of his own sufferings.
An old, poor man who feels the presence of God
stirring his beard. Oh, it would be good
to be again a true believer. Not Marina,
the poet, who finds nothing left in this world . . .
But the quiet priest who leads the orthodox
as they kneel, those worn candles, sure of their light,
surer that they have everything to die for.

For Dulcimer & Doubled Voice

Because the sadness of the mode rests
   in empty singing between the strings; because
      to have this body's close-knit grain, split heart
of cherry, chambered and echoing, is knowledge
   even the deepest songs barely graze our hands,
      whorls slipping away in quiet water
as the bass dive; because the reflections
   of trees lace gray shallows, the pitch and cry
      of marsh light as it quavers, fades, in birch
trunks, sycamore, wooded fretwork marking
   our channel's twisted course; the shores you trace
      beyond us in the haze keep their distance,
vanish, low drone of loss beneath our strokes.
   Silent chorus before the water breaks,
      the quill fallen on the burnished soundboard,
this is ground and air of the river's chant:
   wind turns in the reeds, you tune the dulcimer's
      one doubled chord, and what seemed rooted
in the pattern of vines along these banks
   is undercut by the current's mirrored
      division of each leaf: dissonance
of wake and passage. I watch my image sharpen,
   flare, drifting glaze of sun, a sorrow borne
      away like waves, encircling, spreading outward
beyond what I have left: the body taken
   at last under the keeping of your song.
      If I trust these bearings, if I follow
the white runs as you play, where would we be
   but here, wound in tendrils of the willow,
      you leading my hands along lines of bark,

watersheds passing into watercourses,
   backwaters, as the tree lifts from the minor
     dark of roots, stream, and burdened sky,
to a key where no element is natural
   that does not shift its nature. Curled refrain
     of fog, curved, polished resonance in old wood,
these gestures of grace carry us, and are gone,
   our movement so reflected in the eddying
     distances of the marsh, we seem always
to have just fallen still. As a melody
   repeated on itself becomes the ground
     of silences, as a chart read in scaled
floorboards, in soundings of air, maps a course
   already beneath the hull, we have startled
     a heron from her nest in the cattails
and can only watch her pass, blue and dun pinions
   spread, until the scuddings of dunes and river
     are netted in her flight, forgotten, her cry
driven past the line of sand at the harbor's mouth.
   As we glide through slow water toward our dock.
     Because this is what we're brought to in intervals
of waves: woods and landings; because the current
   flowing toward us and back is a promise
     that what we touch becomes us at last,
moments of song, these splinters swirling
   together in the dulcimer shape of two lovers
     and apart; because we know our lives in the fall
and swell of strings, a sad tuning, still and changed
   to this beauty that gives rise only to itself:
     rings of water, rings of bark, our faces
turning closer; because that is enough.

A Lesson from the Hudson River School: Glens Falls, New York, 1848

(for Dale and Stewart Davis)

It falls by no rule at all; sometimes it leaps, sometimes it tumbles; there, it skips; here, it shoots; in one place 'tis white as snow, and in another 'tis green as grass; hereabouts, it pitches into deep hollows that rumble and quake the 'arth; and thereaway, it ripples and sings like a brook, fashioning whirlpools and gulleys in the old stone, as if 'twas no harder than trodden clay.
James Fenimore Cooper

Look, above the mill-race bridge, the turning wheels . . .
   see how, as the spray flicks, the air
turns bright, laughing, grim and turbulent at once:
a certain blustery quality of light
   not accounted for in paintings
of the old masters. No gothic radiance

   half-hidden by ruins and mist
fills our work, my friend, no glory-haze of Rome
   or Egypt or Greece betraying
some old world's felled stones to our eyes.
No, an American light, as if time stopped
   in the midst of an explosion,

a glass factory, say, and all those splinters
   still hung in the air: hints of death,
to be sure, and hints of a powerful life,
and something more . . . brilliant, scattered reflections,
   as if unfettered souls burst out
to fill this vastness, and the aim of our art

    was but to recollect them. Here,
those pines, if managed with a more precise stroke
      and a greater fidelity
      in your choice of greens, will soon make
the perfect type of *Perseverance* or *Faith*
      in Nature, which is a near thing

to faith in man, faith in yourself. You will learn.
    A style that will become you well
may be found with the same fine taste as your marriage
of a suit and cravat. It is mostly technique,
      though you must still maintain that love
of the unsummoned, unexpected Sublime,

    that trust which has enabled you
to withstand some long hours of eloquence
      at the Lyceum or a jar
      of hard Vermont cider: your hope
that the dregs—of apples or oratory,
      both are dull enough at first taste—

will bless you, as all true gifts bless, suddenly,
    a drunkenness when common hours
seem common no more. You have seen the painting
Sailing above the Narrows, Newburgh, New York?
    I cannot recall the artist,
but he has painted the pleasure fleet racing

    before a line of wooded cliffs,
water and sky both gleaming. It is fine work,
      and particularly because
      one cannot tell if that great glow
comes just before sunset or just after dawn.
    There is a sheen to the sail-cloth

that is almost ghostly, as if the granite
   were some half-forgotten spirit,
his sacrifices gone, his altars broken,
his prayers and hymns unspoken, who yet persists
   in this local revelation,
filling taut canvas with his strong, dappled

   presence, his endless stillness
reflected even by the Hudson's waters.
   Some days the river seems to me
   a rutted cemetery lane,
all those fair sloops running headlong for the rocks,
   the patient watchfulness of shoals . . .

But, to say more of that landscape . . . It recalls
   what Emerson once remarked
we must observe in all the works of genius:
our own rejected thoughts come back, a certain
   alienated majesty.
Although it was not majesty struck me most,

   but a sort of desolation—
all that light caught forever in the pine boughs,
   bound between the stones and current,
   the boats still in their still motion—
nothing like the elegant testimonies
   of the great English Romantics

to time's equally elegant ravages.
   (No, I suspect the truth is this:
that for the Europeans no thoughts remain,
concealed or otherwise. All their pictures
   may reveal to us are remnants,
split husks, forms without the mainspring of spirit.

    Theirs is an art of spectators,
as if their society had reached its height
    with the invention of the clock,
    and then consecrated itself
to the observation, classification,
    and collection of bits of gear,

the torn dials, bent hour-hands littering their hills.)
    But, to return to our painting . . .
to yours, I mean. If you would sketch the full strength
of these rapids, you must not omit the shades
    of slate, blue-gray, even black,
which are not adequately explained away

    as reflections of the mill-wheels,
or as traces of the ore-flecked stream bottom,
    but must be some strange property
    of the river, an illusion
caused by the speedy passage of the current
    through our more constant line of sight.

The source of the Hudson? It lies further north,
    near Marcy. No, I think no one
has yet lugged his paintbox and easel so far,
though to sketch the famous *Opalescent Gorge*,
    as it is called—the whole spectrum
rushing toward you as long as the sunlight lasts,

    and at night, or so I have heard,
a varied glow, like a thousand true moonstones,
    a never failing light—that sight,
    rendered for good on your canvas,
would be worth a few difficult miles of trail.
    I heard once of a man who tried.

A Boston man, he was neither an artist
   nor a woodsman, just a dabbler
in trade, in shipping, in stocks and capital,
who, after losing his townhouse in a fire,
   decided for no clear reason
to purchase a rucksack, paintbrushes, a gun,

   and start for the Adirondacks.
He took the train this far, then started on foot
   and, within a day, lost himself.
   You've seen how the turnpike dwindles,
first a clear trail, then a deer-path, then nothing
   but brambles, windfalls, rippling sounds

that no one has quite explained—they make you think
   the stream must still be near at hand
when you may have strayed far from its banks. He strayed,
stumbled on stumps, fell headlong in a ravine,
   which he followed in the late dusk
until a light began to flicker nearby.

   Through the pine boughs he saw a house,
which, even at some distance, seemed familiar.
   There was no path, no sign of life,
   except, hanging from the front gate,
a lamp, which he recognized as an heirloom
   by the initials in the brass:

his initials, his father's, his grandfather's.
   He stepped back, and saw that the stones,
the brass door plate, the angle of the chimneys,
even the hinges and shutter bolts, belonged
   to his ruined Boston mansion.
He was a practical man. He went inside,

    lit the parlor lamp he purchased
not two years before, pulled a few unread books
    from his shelves, and went up to bed.
    He felt some slight apprehension
of ghosts of his servants who died in the fire,
    but he slept soundly all the same.

What frightened him at last was this: next morning,
    on a tray of antique silver
which had once held the calling cards of his guests,
he found an unbound, half-tattered manuscript,
    written in a hand like his own.
It was *his* history. He read it twice through,

    shuddered, and threw it on the fire.
It was not what was written there that scared him—
    if that volume told him the truth,
    he would return soon to Boston's
wealthy, complacent bosom—but what was not.
    There was no first or last chapter,

no accounting for his birth or for his death . . .
    No, I could hardly swear to you
that the tale is true, nor can I remember
where I first heard it. From my father, perhaps,
    or in that tavern in Glens Falls
where we stopped last night. Maybe it came to me

    as I was walking, a day dream
given in the mesh of branches, root, and sky,
    reflected in the rushing stream—
    the branches gnarled, heavy with moss,
ancient, broken roots, and the current frozen
    in their web. You see, what scares me

about this landscape is that nothing is new,
   nothing forgotten, nothing lost,
and nothing changes. There is no end to it.
Even our ghosts are not souls back from heaven
   or hell. No, they are the stories
we have once heard or told and cannot escape,

   those poor, wandering vestiges
of our thoughts, those accidental reflections,
   illegitimate brain-children,
   whose conception we may deny,
but whom we cannot ever disinherit.
   Well, I have strayed far indeed

from the subject at hand. You do the mill-wheels
   well enough; with more persistence
they may become symbolical of something,
if only of your native strain of talent:
   endless gestures pointing nowhere
but toward yourself. You may rely on that.

*Sometime in the Twenties: A Photograph Never
Found in the Mansion of a Man
Dead by His Own Hand*

Her sort of face has gone a little out of style.
   The palms in the conservatory, leaves
and shade, the long dapplings of ferns across her cheek,
   I hope held you with her awhile. I hope

you saw she was not quite a flirt, and thought her slight,
   odd smile, her lace scarf caught around her throat,
her voice breathy as lace, were not a coy girl's props,
   were more gifts than promises. You let your hand

graze her bare shoulder, let it fall. An accident,
   perhaps. But did you wish you were more bold
than usual, and did you wish you were less sure
   you'd turn away, always the best of hosts,

to other guests? Or, granted a moment's grace
   by breeding or manners, did you press farther,
ask her husband's name, his job, praise him, touch her hand
   in offering a glass, in offering

her yet another view of the ornamental stonework,
   the English maze, the still, formal garden
you so loved. You touched her, say. Well, what of it?
   How could she know what so slight a touch

might intend? And how could she share your dull relief
   as you stepped away, hands in your pockets,
counting the brass keys to your office, roadster,
   greenhouse. Not one key unaccounted for,

none out of place. No old keys, skeletons, too large,
   their plating worn away from opening
how many half-furnished rooms, all those addresses scattered
   in less kindly remembered parts of town.

Where else could you two meet? Her cab a block ahead,
   her new pale coat, earrings like shattered ice
(it's winter now), she turns down Joseph Avenue
   or Gregory Street. And then a hall, then doors,

and bulbs, flickering and dusty, and immigrant voices, harsh,
   thick, smell of sausage, then stairs to Number Twelve
or Eight, the stubborn lock, the same green bedspread, musty,
   close, your calf and gold appointment book

caught somewhere in the sheets. None of this ever happened.
   You counted keys. You caught her eye, almost,
and saw, your shadow on her cheek, how these things end.
   The library phone rings. You stand or sit

or stare past rose-lined walks and wait for someone's voice
   to say you are engaged or ill or not
receiving calls, and so on through the little slights
   your servants learn to give, through awkward partings,

awkward scenes, at awful parties, at worse hotels.
   She sends this picture with her compliments.
And that is all. No, at most you touched her once,
   and the photograph is just the gift

of a friend, a slight good friend. You've turned away,
   the best of hosts, and rich enough to trust
your taste for foregone conclusions and omitted sins,
   your world offering so much to refuse.

A Side of Beef

Chaim Soutine, 1925

I have sent the girl to the butcher's again.
She is not fit
for anything more than this little sketch, too plain
not to forget with the rest: a white
receding figure with streaks of weak umber and sienna
who fetches blood in a shallow earthenware basin.
Perhaps if she saw her face reflected there,
ochre broken over vermillion,
she would become interesting.
Perhaps the smell on the stairs might make her stagger, a little.

And this would be the beginning of desire: my unpainted
self-portrait as a boy in a winter village
who shivers against the slaughterhouse wall
and prays for the warmth of a carcass hung over damp straw.

Once, I learned that of the thousand ways to gut a fowl,
only that one is sacred
which allows the soul to vanish without flutterings or cries.
I, who no longer believe the dead find peace,
except for a moment
when they take leave of fear with a little wave, a shrug,
as I might see a friend off on a short and routine journey . . .

So I have come to love the body on the edge of ascension:
a peasant woman, say, posed beneath a bridge, with her pale shift
hiked almost to her thighs, who stops screaming
and watches the lightning flare, the river grip her legs.
There is a little truth
where she hangs between fire and water, a stillness
that lasts only so long as the soul cannot choose its element.

(I left out the bridge, rocks in a gray light, those gnarled limbs,
to show, in her face,
the heart of nature: two notes, clear
and close and dissonant,
that will never resolve themselves.)

To have faith in this is to live much of the time in poverty.
What money there is
goes for a side of beef delivered fresh each morning.
By noon it will have lost those pigments
which are not the semblance of life, but the whole of it.

Then Paulette will return with her basin full
and bathe the carcass
in whatever blood the butcher did not need for sausage.
In this she is the greater artist.
She gags, her features twist, her hands and dress are spattered,
but she has that skill I envy in boxers in the ring
when their fists draw color to a bruise.

I, who can only copy, as Homer did, the vigil
we keep to summon the dead,
those great imaginings . . . They tell us only what we know:
that hell is a dry, unpleasant place
where heroes and heroes' mothers go thirsty.
But when their lips first lap
our sacrifice, when their faces take on shape and flush,
somewhere, I think, there must be a boy who walks from great
                                                                          cold
into a room where lamplight plays
across slaughtered cattle. Their hides transfigured
in the afterimage
of leather and a guttering lantern: on a blue ground,
ochre and vermillion.

Mount Hope: To Weldon Kees

So many went away and left no word. The detective forgot the
   crime, the clues; where he ran along the warehouses by the river
   there is only a stain of soot, like a man's shape running, washing
   away in the rain.
The ad-man checked his tie, his watch, counted the bottles above
   the bar in Eddie's Chop House one more time. He died, I heard,
   with an empty briefcase beside him on the Broad Street bus.
Even my great-grandfather, who they said was a talkative man,
   who ran the livery stable on an avenue gone now to tenements,
   settlement houses, turned his face to the wall, having made his
   last confession in low German to a priest who did not under-
   stand.

They are all here, forgotten now, in Mount Hope, where hope, if it
   goes on, goes on in silence, because it is January and the wind
   carries away the sounds of the few walkers.
I came here to find the graves of my mother's family, those hos-
   tlers, lens-grinders, lathe mechanics. But what could I ask of
   them?
I do not think they wait for me over drinks in some heaven like the
   drawing rooms of the mansions on East Avenue, nor do they
   reach out in the boughs of these winter lilacs. And I do not envy
   the dead who keep their places and have no voices left,

As I envy you, your silhouette half seen on the beach in a winter
   fog. You seem, in your reserve, imperishable. And your ques-
   tions—*What words What answers now?*—were forgiveness enough
For my halting answer. Which was to say there were worse ends
   than yours and to believe a man might well turn away, from the
   living and from the dead, and lose himself in his words

As in the harsh smoke of a room where you or I might sit at a corner table, alone, and light a cigarette, while no one plays on the piano some sad forties riff.

And the sheet music on the band-stand, those phrases you do not hear and cannot forget . . . How they persist. *What memories What ruined harbors?*

A Lost Sonata

Stockholm, December 1904

    Beloved,
  you must remember how you came
to me each night before our marriage; surely
what so wrenched my soul was no mere dream. I tried
  always to push away your vision,
  but everywhere there was a scent
    I could not place: stale,
  sweet, private, it woke around me
like a deep mist, and even as I slept flame
  leapt to my hands and seared the letters

    of your name
  across the headboard. We painted
the room yellow to hide our dread of a child.
You have broken the glass figure of Jason
  and said I am not a proper man.
  Well, what are you but another
    creature of scent, blood,
  the hollowness that leaves a man
nothing but his lesser self: a child crying
  for forgiveness under his mother's

    hand. So much
  for the summer light streaked across
your breast. I have no right to repent, and no
desire, and so have preferred always twilight,
  my great oak table where I divide
  myself from these shards, your spirit.
    The rending of flesh
  is one solace. Again last night

books fell of their own accord from the shelves, knives
   lay in the design of a womb, while

      your shadow
   kept its watch over what little is left
between me and my death. Will you not leave me
a few more days of peace? Will you not come back?
   Except to you, who have gathered
   more of my past than ever I
      would wish to recall,
   I do not write. I sit, carve meat
from the joint as if it were my heart's shriving,
   and bear only that music which plays on

      fewest strings.
   Listen, the small cannons firing
from the Horse Guards' camp, are they not like a song
half remembered: *Tod . . . Tod . . .* It was Aspasia
   who sang, while her husband smoked and laughed
   like a drunkard at the keyboard.
      Staczu! He knew she
   was Bengt's, was Munch's, was mine, and still
he played his damned Schumann *Aufschwung* again,
   again, while our carnival

      wheel danced on
   through his bed. If you have never
seen Munch's portrait of him, as if dismembered,
his face lost in her hair, it is no matter.
   You are her, or close enough. And just
   so were Siri, Frida . . . The one,
      a whore, remembered
   her baron with her lips when I
had put him out of mind; the other, pregnant,
   forced me at last to alchemy,

    Inferno,
  a stone boiling within a stone.
Slut, mother of madness . . . And you, whose spirit
summons them all, as if it were fit calling
    for me to walk among the shades of those
    I would die gladly to forget.
      I tried to poison
  my little daughter by magic
so Frida and I could join hands at her death-
  bed and be happy again. Oh yes,

      guilt and fear
  are what we marry, and marriage
is a serious affair, not soon given up.
A bond to all we love. In the afternoon,
    I thought I would walk again across
    the bridge to the birch woods, and not
      think of you at all.
  But on all sides the broken stumps
rose from the snow, small skulls of children left here
  in a story to die as payment

      for those sins
  their parents loved. I felt again
fear that I would die of a slow perishing
from drink, my life settle like a cigar ash
    at the heart of a brandy well past
    its prime, a low, rancid grace note
      of decay. Just then
  I stumbled on a root so gnarled
it seemed the map of a country where all hope,
  all wanderers must fail; each road led

      my single
  strand to a net so intricate

no lifetime is enough for separation.
I followed, as best I could, a gully
   where the path led downward through remnants
   of heather. Among crevasses
      left by streams now dry
   or choked with rocks, I lost my way,
or what little way I had, and a new snow
   began, worse than any I have seen,

      if vision
   can be the word for what led me
alone to blindness. First, a few flakes, barely
present, like a spider's nest, the scarves of lace
   and silk you draped over my eyes;
   there was no wind but this white breath.
      Then the world changed,
   swirled, and grew blank. If through a crack
in the storm, I saw the face of Siri's poor
   dead baby, or heard the Pole's rough hands

      play again
   the melody of a sadness
meant to poison the souls of his wife's lovers,
it was only for a moment. The fever
   grew with the snow, and I felt my whole
   body a nest of flame. I stood
      still, burning! Nothing
   moved around me, and everything.
Wherever I reached out, I felt a presence
   that would not yield to my hand:

      a great stone,
   chipped and marred where I touched its face.
I traced out the runes, the ruins, of your name
and mine where before there had been only snow,

and knew if I followed you farther
down this path what I would become
   at last: memory
only, my own or yours, useless
as the images in a graveyard: death's head,
   cherub, chorus of grinning eunuchs

     giving birth
to themselves over and over.
There was no way back. I prayed quickly, plunged
once more toward the end of this damp, female
   mask which hid the world's familiar ground
in its white veil, perfumed
     with a scent I now
remembered, smell of celery,
of a bone broken off at the root. The snow
   turned even my breath against me; frost

     gripped my throat,
   a taste of raw spirits. I woke,
and the storm had passed. Above me, a huge tree,
a silver ash, rose higher from the new drifts
   even than my great joy at seeing
   how many leaves could fall away,
     each revealing
   in its loss, in the branched fretwork
of its veins, some trace of this quiet beauty.
   As if confession could not only

     ease a death,
   but render it simple as speech,
a passage from one person to another,
I told my life in a litany of limbs
   as I climbed and came finally

to a place where I was nothing
   but the shuddering
of branches in the air, frightened
for the first time by neither my history
   nor its end, but only that the wind

      might soon cease.
   It was over all too soon. First,
I felt the foolishness of a man too old
to be caught dangling above the ground, then lights
   glimmered from the town, a distant call
   I never could ignore; their warmth
      was what I have loathed
   and craved always: the lives of men
with ears to hear and minds to misinterpret.
   You see now why we fear any birth:

      a child is
   ourselves come back, wrong, misshapen,
and bears our name for life; it is horrible
to think we might live forever. If I write
   to you like a man whittling himself
   away, it is my memory
      at fault. Its gesture
   has always been toward tragedy,
the paring down of opposites through details.
   And if each life I summon, each scene,

      must wound me
   into strength enough to devour
what I love, so in speaking I find myself
at last forgetting. When I reached home, I saw
   the table, which last night split from end
   to end, was healed, and the dinner
      bones were scattered just

    as I left them. Let the lawyers
finish their work. We are divorced, and omens
   mean nothing now but that things end.
                                              Yours,
  Strindberg

An Apology for Loving the Old Hymns

Through a church window in Livonia, New York,
last night I heard again the only hymn
I ever got by heart,
When I Survey That Wondrous Cross, whose theme
is pride grown bright, turned bitter, ragged, fallen,
as the ash leaves turn
from flame to smudge to spent ash, and the half-
stained sky turns cloudy, turns away. What broke
among those voices but
their harsh self-love; what splintered grain of song,
rasp of unbarked walnut boughs, split
the organ reeds, woodwind
and horn stops overblown, if not some music
older than all that congregation, seasoned
by more harsh weathering,
a score of limbs windblown on a frozen creek.

Listen, I told myself, as the road bore west
and gravel danced and fell
under the truck, this isn't winter yet.
The autumn fires still smoulder by the roadside.
Yet all this year you've found
such pride, too much, in the work of your hands,
and through this early frost, the windows branched
and fogged, all you can see
are ruined fields and worn barns, their planks sprung,
patched with tin scraps, gone in the joists,
the hunter's dull red moon
kindling the crosspieces.
                         And my own house,

the house I built, well-timbered, plumb . . . I found
no joy in the thought of it,
only that half-expectant peace you feel, head bowed,
after the choir has stopped, and still you're sure
the verses will just go on,
sure of the words: *my richest gain I count
a loss, and pour contempt on all my pride.*
One hand on the gearshift,
stopped, mouthing those words, *my richest
gain I count a loss*, wishing them empty
of everything but music,
feeling the truck shiver as the wind rose,
I stepped from the cab and stood a minute, hunched
against the swell, moved
a little by its barren, persistent refrain,
moved again by the lull as the gusts turned north.

Remember, I asked myself,
that pause before the hymn's last chord,
how the tenor draws one long breath and turns
for a moment toward the pews,
filled with the pride his voice is given, sure
that gift is beyond his measure. Loose on its latch,
the door blew open,
and on the varnished floor the shadow of a maple
I'd planted bowed and straightened again,
like a man who knows
his songs will end as the broken voice of branches
and yet still wants the last word sung
to be a blessing: *amen.*

PART TWO
A Mirror for Loyalists

*Being
a Portrait
by Several Hands
of the Late Sir William Johnson
Baronet
Royal Superintendent of Indian Affairs
& Proprietor of Johnson Hall
Tryon County, New York
1715-1774
Deo Regique Debito*

Walter Butler: Dispatches from the Mohawk Frontier, 1778

(for John Drury)

We ware just now informed by an Oneyda Indian,
that yesterday an Onandago Indian arrived at one of the branches
of the Susquehana called the Tioga,
that he was present at a great meeting of Indians
and Tories at that place and their result was to attack Charevalley,
and that young Butler was to lead the Tories.
I send you this information that you may be on your guard.

the commander of Fort Stanwix to
Colonel Alden, commander of the garrison
at Cherry Valley, November 6th, 1778

Niagara, October 25th

Major John Butler, Chief Commander,
   His Majesty's Rangers, &ct., &ct. Sir:
      I am most sensible of the just
         preferment extended me

under your generous patronage
   since I escaped the traitors' confines
      at Albany. There is some small truth
         in tales that I broke my word,

first in requesting that my parole
   be in the care of one Richd. Cartwright,
      a secret friend of the King's great cause,
         who kept his barn door unlatched

and his horse ever groomed for my use,
   and again, in taking advantage

of this convenience, though I had sworn
   I would neither attempt flight

nor seek to rejoin the King's service.
   I suffer no remorse. My oath, given
      amidst threats and duress to traitors,
         would never be held binding

save by that same mob, who have trampled
   their own sworn loyalty under foot,
      and that for a most petty quarrel
         over taxes. Let them call

us *damn'd Tories*, or whate'er they please;
   let them tar and feather our servants,
      steal our plate, turn our Anglican pews
         to tavern stools and kindling;

we bear such distinctions with honor.
   Sir, I am forsworn, but to base men
      whose rebellion drives e'en God abroad
         and sets virtue a-whoring.

What gallows-rebel could with justice
   demand my word? Thus I do remain
      a gentleman and your son. My thanks
         for my present rank are due,

and are as much a son's pious thanks
   for the inheritance of a taste
      and genius for the sword as they are
         a soldier's. And yet I must ask you,

Father, to refrain from seasoning
   your letters with such admonitions

       as these following, of which in truth
          I stand in but little need.

My son, you write, *have no relations*
   save the most exclusive with those tribes
      under your command. The dignity
         of an English officer

is sorely tried in any dispute
   with a savage, and as for friendship,
      I do not believe any white man,
         since the much regretted death

of Sir William Johnson, has eyes clear
   enough, or sympathies various
      enough, to conceive what such a word
         might mean in the wilderness

of a Mohawk's sensibilities.
   You must maintain that sober pride
      proper to your rank, if you would win
         their respect. Sir, I would not,

need not concern myself with winning
   what I already command by right
      of rank if not by right of birth nor—
         need I remind you of this,

who first catechized me?—by virtue
   of that greater participation
      in the divine perfection granted
         to all civilized nations.

If man, as we are taught, is God's mirror,
   I think it no heresy to add

      that glass shares more of His grace which yields
        such an image as our own.

Observe a Mohawk, and you will see
   neither harmony nor proportion
      nor any other divine aspect,
        but only the dim image

a man might see in an antique mirror,
   its silver peeled, held to the window,
      so the very wilderness seems mixed
        with his features, as if God

had not yet made man to stand apart
   from the brutes, nor even from the rocks.
      As for your most discrete suggestion
        that I *avoid all carnal*

connections with women of the tribes,
   I tell you, Sir, I would as soon try
      a vixen or a she-bear in rut.
        It is sound warning enough

to recall how Johnson's savage wife
   mourned that noble baronet's passing
      by kicking a prisoner's scalped head
        round her room in this fortress,

mingling, all the while, insults with shrill
   endearments, as if vengeance and lust
      coupled in her wailings. I would swear
        it was as if Niagara's

stones had returned to their native cliffs
   and were overgrown again with briars

       and maples as ruddy as new-killed
          venison. And then her cries,

again and again, as if great wolves
    swarmed along the ridge trail, running down
        some poor hunter and his famished mount.
           And then the awful clatter

as the head struck a rack of fire tools.
    With such scenes ever before my eyes,
        I think you need not fear too greatly
           for my chastity, nor fret

that, like Sir William, I should become
    a savage, as it were, by marriage,
        my heart trapped like his in that chaos
           which nature is without men

who serve—as we do, as do all true
    Englishmen—the divine and royal
        end of subordinating this world
           to ordered will. Albany

and the Mohawk castles are, at heart,
    alike as only two Hells may be,
        haunts of devils who scorn all laws save
           that hunger of old Chronos,

who, in the act of generation,
    insured his glut of cod and belly
        alike. *The Mohawks are our allies,*
           we their fathers, you write. Sir,

for a time. But like the first Titans,
    and like these upstart Boston cowards,

>   they will vanish soon enough. And we
>   will make this world a heaven yet.
>
>   Your loyal son and servant,
>
>   *Captain Walter Butler*

Tioga, November 1st

Major John Butler, &ct., &ct. Dear Sir:
   If I have not swallowed your advice
      quite whole, if I ventured to amend
         your letter's paternal text

with some few conclusions from my own
   engagements in this western country,
      these are no grounds on which to charge me
         with lack of filial respect.

Respect is one thing; obsequious
   gutter-crawling is a traitor's game,
      not proper between father and son.
         My respect for your orders

has compelled me on to Tioga
   for a rendezvous with Joseph Brant
      (I cannot call him *Captain*; his nose-
         pendant gives that rank the lie)

when I would as soon meet with vipers
   on a narrow trail in all the rage
      and venom of their coupling. So much
         bad ink has spilled in Brant's praise,

an unwary man might think this *great*
   Savage fit for Christian company.
      It near sickened me to see him play
         the courtier in London,

to see the finely bred court ladies
   break the ranks of their quadrille and run
      for a glimpse of him, to hear poets
         praise his eyes (which seem to me

no more majestic than the stone bed
   of a stream just before the rapids:
      hard, featureless, and little worthy
         of trust). I consoled myself

with the thought that a peeress might stare
   with as much interest at a fox
      run to ground and worried by the hounds,
         or at a wild boar, caught, caged,

and brought to cry his rutting bellow
   through King George's halls. Brant is not tame;
      indeed, for all his feigned gentleness,
         when he entered those fine rooms

and stood by the fire to light his pipe
   with a coal caught on his scalping knife,
      it was as if his red uniform
         and all the silk wall hangings,

the embroidered crests and gilt armor,
   the very palace walls, fell away
      and we stood in their council chamber
         at Onandaga, shivering

under a chinked bark roof and sweating
   under some sachem's stare, like poor souls
      caught between Satan's flames and the ice-
         rent void. Sir, although you say

that Brant has learned much of our ways,
   I see only that he has acquired
      that arrogance which most common men
         affect when they have presumed

to a station not properly theirs.
   It gives me no small pain to report
      that some ninety Loyalist rangers,
         having served long months with Brant,

have gone so far astray from their oaths
   of service as to desert my force,
      after claiming that I insulted them
         by refusing to return Brant's salute

and that my *grave lack of discretion
and tact*—their words, Sir, when I declined
      to dine with that Mohawk in his tent
         or to grant his insolent

demand that he take an equal part
   in planning the attack—endangered
      the sure success of our enterprise.
         Those traitors are better gone.

This is how matters stand: Brant's Mohawks—
   whose loyalty seems yet firm, although
      their captain is as fierce and sullen
         as his vast reputation

would paint him subtle and dignified—
   are encamped on the wood's edge, while I
     and my own Rangers (whose love for Brant
       is even less than your son's)

have pitched our tents and raised the King's flag
   on the ruins of an Iroquois town
     but lately razed by a rebel force.
       Perhaps this will amuse you:

Late last night, an ancient savage stalked
   without announcement into my tent
     and in his own tongue—of which I know
       little and could understand

still less, so faintly did I attend
   and so mixed was his discourse with sobs,
     groans, and the like—began an account
       of the sack of Tioga

at the hands of Col. Hartley's rebels.
   The cruelty of their militia
     seemed believable enough, and yet
       I could scarce credit the grief

of this man at losing what surely
   amounted to no more than a few shacks,
     a few plots of corn. (As for his claim
       that at Onaquaga town

the Iroquois lost some forty houses,
   log houses, mind you, with stone chimneys
     and glass windows, to a rebel raid,
       that was an old man's dream, no more.)

I stopped his clamorous cries—whether
   of rage or mourning I could not tell—
      by feigning sleep and, hearing him leave,
         prepared to rest in earnest,

when I felt a hand on my shoulder.
   I did not mention—nor much notice,
      so great my outrage at his visit—
         that this Indian's daughter

had accompanied him. She was fair
   enough for a savage, with good teeth
      and broad, supple shoulders, and she sat
         with a trained hunter's patience

through all his endless, broken lament.
   You may have guessed, given your great knowledge
      of these licentious forest women,
         what was afoot. The old man

took his leave, but not the girl. Her hand
   slipped down from my shoulder toward my belt
      (I always sleep full-dressed, as becomes
         an officer in the field),

stopping first to loosen the brass buttons
   of my tunic, but never finished
      its mission. I am a man, and felt
         as a man, not as a beast

who knows nothing more of the trap's bait
   than that its sweetness sets mouth and brain
      swimming alike. I pinioned her arms,
         hoisted her out of my cot,

and threw her from the tent. Do you guess
   what saved me? I thought of Sir William,
      whose pleasure in wilderness slatterns
         was a general scandal.

(Even in London there were rumors
   he was father to several hundred
      mongrel brats.) We know the Spanish pox
         added filthy agonies

to those conscience must have inflicted
   had he been as much a good Christian
      as he was a devout worshipper
         of his own prideful powers

of generation. Yet such powers
   are common to the rankest marsh weed,
      to the viper, the tent louse; indeed
         the grimmest plague is no more

than this force of Priapus, thrusting
   one species beyond all bounds, their numbers
      swelling until they have overrun
         their hosts. Until the English

are as numerous as the Iroquois,
   siring half-breeds seems a traitor's work.
      Far too often, on these New York raids,
         behind leaves or in the charred

wreck of a farmhouse, or when the reeds
   shake like dry bones though there is no wind,
      I feel the presence of Johnson's pups,
         whose dark and mixed loyalties

are given neither to our good King,
   nor to the chiefs, but to an empire
      swept clean of both, where no division
         holds twixt man and that spirit

which sets all nature afire and turns
   our civilization's works to mere
      decorations in a burning hall
         where warriors feast and tup

and fill their maws, and are hardly more
   human than the great flames raging there.
      Such are our allies. Sir, we use them
         as much to our lasting shame

as to our victory. I tell you,
   it was not simple fear of the pox
      kept me off that wanton, but the thought
         of old Sir William's bastard,

young William of Canajoharie,
   who ran, with two pistols and a sword
      and a stolen British uniform,
         through a rebel town, screaming

I am a King's man. Have I not killed
   Yankees already at Fort St. John
      with my father's sword? I have killed them,
         scalped them, and kicked their arses,

and will cut off your own heads by and by!
   I would not be father to *that*, Sir,
      nor to any bloody vanity,
         nor, save for your orders,

would I lead Little Billy, Half Town,
   Cornplanter, Farmer's Brother, Blacksnake,
      Twenty Canoes, Onongadaka,
         Hohnogwus, Wundungoteh . . .

Hear those names, like a trail beginning
   at a meadow's edge that leads you
      through a wood lot, then to denser trees,
         past rapids and falls, up hill,

along a granite ridge, and then at last
   leaves you to wander at the cliff edge,
      to stare at the howling chasm below.
         These Mohawks are not concerned

with what lies nearest to our hearts: the just
   retribution a king's officers
      exact from rebels, not in the name
         of vengeance but of honor,

and with an anger as calm, refined,
   and impersonal as God's wrath. No,
      we share nothing. Have you not wondered
         as you watched the fire kindled

in their camp and heard their cries or heard
   their endless, garbled oratory,
      or searched their faces where nature's rage
         and savage treachery writhe,

if they are not like those damned spirits
   of old children's tales, who lurk in mirrors
      and make a man mistrust his features
         because their deformed masks seem

    to tell his character more truly?
        This is the worst temptation, to fear
            some connection may exist between
                their race and ours. Resist it!

It is only in the dimmest firelight
    that such correspondences seem true.
        In full daylight, these heretic thoughts,
            like fornications, are clear

cases of faith brought low by nature
    and stink to heaven. The Iroquois
        are not safe pawns, never true consorts.
            They have their own occasions.

        Your loyal son and servant,

        Captain Walter Butler

Niagara, December 6th

Major John Butler, &ct. Dear Father:
    You ask for *a full account, truthful*
        in all particulars, of the raid,
            that you may confound rumors,

presently abroad among our troops,
    that paint my conduct in a *wanton*
        and vicious light. Peace, my father, peace.
            My report is on its way,

and I draft this private testimony
    solely to relate some incidents,
        too minor for official notice,
            but which may serve to restore

your faith in your son's gift of command.
   First I would refute the whispered charge
      that I was unable to restrain
         the Iroquois in their rage,

having forfeited all obedience
   through mere callous arrogance and spleen.
      Sir, I was no friend to the tribesmen,
         but that was not my purpose,

nor was it your advice. A captain
   who would lead Indians cannot speak
      to his troops of honor, duty, King,
         for how can those savages

translate words that in their own rough tongue
   are voids, chasms, ambuscades in empty woods,
      meaningless . . . Nor can he hope to win
         respect from them, save that stern,

forced trust a stone yields to the mason.
   Some days before we reached Tioga,
      I was approached by one *brave*—a word
         not without its humor here,

since this Red Jacket was widely known
   for a coward who preferred the hind-
      most battle lines. (One common tale claims
         that he was given his name

because he once stole a scarlet coat
   from a drunken sergeant and then swore
      he won it in a bout of wrestling
         with our Sir William Johnson,

to whom, in their second match, he lost
   only his old leggings.) Red Jacket
      strode up to my seat before the fire,
         and vowed he would march no more

in our service while his own village
   lay unprotected and his wife's crops
      might be ravaged by the militia.
         He complained yet further that

he had hardly time to hunt, though furs
   grew ever scarcer and no longer
      bought needful things, since our white traders,
         having turned soldier, would pay

only for the scalps of the rebels.
   In truth, I know of no such bounties
      (though both Sir William and our French foes
         in the old fight thus enticed

their Indian allies to acts of war),
   and I told Red Jacket that he lied
      in painting us so barbarously,
         and added that his duty

lay with the King, his father and friend.
   (I maintained throughout that calm reserve
      you commended to me.) He replied
         that, bounties or no, the truth

was that no Englishman would give aid
   to an Indian who did not fight,
      and that the rebels were no different,
         and that Sir William Johnson

(whom he called by his Indian name,
   Warraghiyagey) would have disowned
      his white children, had he known their hands
         would wield the covenant chain

as a lash to force the Senecas
   to fight the Oneidas, their brothers
      in the League of the Six Nations.
         I might have reminded him

how Johnson played off one wretched tribe
   against another for years until all
      their sachems' heads were set a-spinning
         by his schemes, and he alone,

an old spider dozing in his web,
   was a still point where their eyes might rest.
      But Red Jacket grabbed me by the coat,
         tore my Ranger-green lapel,

and scoffed that Johnson had never worn
   English clothes for Indian affairs.
      I saw no profit in more speech.
         I loosed my scabbard, swung it high,

and offered to give him the whipping
   his conduct merited, but he fled
      and a few friends with him. The Mohawks
         muttered awhile together,

but did not desert—a certain sign
   that the greater my severity,
      the more their awe increased. The next charge,
         that I allowed the Indians

to attack the town, knowing full well
  that they were intent on butchery
    inspired by long-rankling grievances,
      is little more than slander.

That Blacksnake made a great oration
  and declared that the Yankees were liars
    to accuse his Senecas of the cruel
      slaughter of women and boys

during the Wyoming Valley raids,
  but he would make honest men of them
    at Cherry Valley; that Little Beard—
      angry that rebel captives

granted parole by him had forsworn
  their oaths of peace, joined the militia,
    and raided the tribal villages—
      cursed and said never again

would he give quarter to an enemy . . .
  such rumors abound in all armies,
    and seldom reach a commander but
      as half-heard, fragmented tales.

What officer has time to sift truth
  from a broken wilderness of lies,
    savage gutterals, misshapen forms
      stalking through his encampment?

My duty was to our good King's wrath,
  not to interpret some Mohawk's screech,
    nor to order the flames into a hymn,
      nor to make the granite ledges

form ranks and dance a civil measure.
   These Iroquois have lived forever
      and brought no order to their country
         nor to themselves. To tame them,

one must first descend into their chaos.
   Johnson tried, and was made a Mohawk
      for his pains, an honor too much like
         damnation to suit my taste.

Lastly, I have been taken to task
   for my failure to halt the carnage.
      Sir, when I saw the bloody hatchets
         of the Iroquois, and smoke

above the homes of those Loyalists
   who were our spies in Cherry Valley,
      and whose property was to be spared
         by your orders, my dismay

and my anger were so great that I fell
   at the foot of a tree, half a-swoon
      and half boiling over, as if rage
         scorched my reason near away,

and my sight must have dimmed with fever,
   for I dreamt I sat in Johnson Hall,
      across the table from Sir William,
         who wore the patched buck leggings

an Indian trapper wears in snow,
   and the red jacket of a soldier,
      and a brass gorget hung with feathers.
         His legs were overgrown with vines,

and his face was near eaten away
   by two hordes of ants, one scarlet troop
      and one a deepest earthen russet.
         They battled over his flesh.

His shoulders were so vast they split the walls,
   and yet he shook; grief and fear mingled
      as he called in a thin voice, wasted,
         my children, oh my children . . .

I awoke to screams nearby, shuddered,
   shook my head, picked an axe from the ground,
      and crept toward a cabin, where I feared
         some settler's girl was near death.

As I opened the door, the screaming
   changed to a laugh, then a strange giggling.
      A mirror, framed in cherry wood, was propped
         on a low table, tilted

so I could see the reflection
   of the woman standing before it,
      apparently admiring her dress
         (of finer material

than is common in the frontier towns,
   an English print) and a cloth bonnet
      which completely hid her hair and neck.
         You know I am not a man

of sudden passions. If I was stirred,
   it was but by the thought of saving
      one Christian soul from death's ravishment.
         I called. She giggled again,

but there was something horrible in it,
   low and throaty, like a man gagging
      on his own blood. I called more loudly,
         and when she seemed not to hear,

I reached with my free hand to touch her
   and felt hard muscle beneath the dress.
      It was no girl. I raised the hatchet,
         and when the head turned toward me,

and I saw an Indian's features,
   I brought it down, grazed the skull, and cut
      the left shoulder, just below the neck.
         He fell, spat, looked up. Again

giggling, this time with blood in earnest,
   and I recognized him: a half-wit
      Mohawk, deaf and near dumb, who haunted
         our camp and was driven off

just before our force left Tioga.
   He cringed at my feet, scraped his torn face
      along my boot; his body doubled
         and stretched inside the fine dress,

like some poor girl shaken on the spit
   of an unwonted passion. And then,
      beneath the bed, I saw the broken
         body of a white woman,

her fine dark hair near torn off her head.
   I gagged, and swung my axe high again,
      when from the maelstrom of his whimpers
         a sort of singing noise came,

two syllables, sung again and again,
    as he clutched at my leggings. *Father*,
        he sang it in clear English, *Father* .
            I split his throat nearly through.

Sir, you are at liberty to recount
    this adventure. 'Tis my best defense
        against charges of leniency
            toward the crimes of our allies.

        Your son and loyal servant,

    Captain Walter Butler

Guy Johnson: London, 1788

And in their train, to fill the press,
Come apish Dance, and swoln Excess,
Mechanic Charme, and vicious Taste,
And Fashion in her changing dress.
Hoadley, lines after *The Rake's Progress*

Move the lamp closer. No, no. There. Turn the wick
lower, let there be more shadows. Let them play
across Sir William's portrait. I would see him
    dimly even now,
      as I best recall him,
   his face, part soot and part flame,
    an endless strife. My dead uncle.
Though I say he was like a father to me,
I mean only that he had a father's face,
   if, as the old Greeks proposed, war
   is the father of all things.
     Sons must take their fathers,
      good or ill, whereas

a nephew is free to prefer the comforts
of a blaze to its rage, or features mottled,
like mine, from gin to . . . Boy, another glass here.
    Look, there in his eyes,
      how the paint seems to scale
   and reveal flecks of dull white
   below the green. Those were his eyes,
like snowfall in a deep forest, unsettling
a dappled world of sunlight and earth, setting
   new boundaries, breaking the peace
   between trunk and root. Genius . . .
     he had the Englishman's
     genius for measure,

surveying, just apportionment, stone fences.
He was like a great boulder, run nearly through
with a thousand dark fissures, and yet loving
    his splintered brightness
    more than any clear gem.
  Boy, go to the tavern now,
  fetch another bottle . . . He's gone.
That is what servants do, and nephews, all such
lackeys. They give you a few sidelong glances,
  pilfer a few trifles, and leave
  you to the less than tender
    mercies of memory.
    But, Uncle, perhaps

it is providential that we are alone.
What I could never tell you straight to your face,
because I could never find there one still point
    where my eyes might rest,
    I can say now at last
  to this portrait you so loathed.
  ("The painter," you said, "has made me
seem the worst of all men, a man of fashion.
Stooped, round shoulders . . . and smooth hands! And just look
                                    here,
  how my features almost dissolve
  in the speckled wallpaper.
    No this is hardly me."
    You left it to me.)

If there is one thing I shall never forgive,
it must be that what you valued most in me
was my least gift, my knack for cartography.
    What was my great *Map*
    of the VI Nations but
    the journal of your exploits

    and intrigues, a fresh division
of your life from the lives of lesser mortals;
what were the Iroquois but your household gods;
    the Mohawk clansmen but your hand
    outstretched. What has my life been
      but one endless survey,
      your private preserve.

Hardly a life at all, that of a province
whose glory is the capital's radiance
broken, diffused, into rumors, bad weather,
    poor houses, worse taste.
    And what of my portrait?
  One Canajoharie wit
  said it resembled a certain
baronet's favorite chair: well-stuffed, yielding
to the slightest shifts of your great lordship's weight,
    and that the Mohawk brave standing
    behind me might as well be
      some upholsterer's man
      come for spring cleaning.

Well, had I never forsaken the pencil
for my current retinue of cane, corkscrew,
and catarrh, I'd have drawn my likeness better,
    a death-bed portrait
    in the style of Hogarth:
  a chamber much like this one,
  the chairs broken up for kindling,
empty bottles, the bed groaning on three legs,
a thieving servant, a master with nothing
  left to steal. And a few touches,
  more fanciful, but still true
    to the subject's spirit:
    above the mantel

a caged monkey, half-starved, half-bald, yammering,
and beside him two portraits, paired like Greek masks,
comic and tragic—a stern, elegant Lord,
    and an oversized,
    obsequious fellow,
  whose splendid red uniform
  now graces a Cheapside pawnshop.
A third picture too, I think, a real Hogarth,
Plate V of *The Rake's Progress*: the wastrel heir
  wedding an elderly widow
  for reasons too obvious
    to require my comments.
    Notice how his eyes,

dear Uncle, turn with equally obvious
intent toward the young bridesmaid, and notice too
that a crack runs through the Sixth Commandment's plaque.
    (I suppose the girl
    is the old bride's daughter.)
  I am no stern moralist,
  nor a 'specially moral man,
but is this not a fair representation
of your lust for Molly Brant? She is the girl,
  I mean, who must play the harlot
  while her mother—the Six Nations,
    if I may extend
    my allegory

from the sensual to the political;
you pretended to keep such affairs distinct,
but took your pleasures wherever they might come—
    while her dear mother
    is swived quite royally,
  if, because of her age
  and frank distaste for novelty,

more in spirit than in fact. Her true father—
the longhouse fire, symbol, in my parallel,
  of the ancient fidelity
  of the Iroquois—spent, doused,
    buried by your desire
    to measure her charms

against profits in furs, the King's endless thirst
for allies against the French, the newest wing
of Johnson Hall. You won over the Mohawks,
    sent Joseph to school,
    made him a strange mongrel,
  part Mason, part hatchet-man,
  made Molly your good English whore.
You took their most private gift, the great Valley,
grasped it tight, stripped it, and with a few harsh strokes
  on a royal grant made it yours.
  And, Uncle, even in death,
    you trimmed them down farther,
    dividing their wealth

among us, your will true to its own nature
from first to last. You were true to nothing else.
And your legend, what of that? Well, I have learned
    that it is not myths
    reveal a man, but facts,
  those broken relics of you,
  who were never all of a piece,
you, who always severed ties yet sought firm ground,
made new alliances to see just what lay
  now within, now without your reach.
  A division on a ground
    the musicians call it,
    that was your true style:

a chord, then endless variations, hinting
now at this new modulation, now at that,
and each more refined, more rigorous, more stale.
    So your heirs have turned
      on each other in court
    over an inheritance
    long gone to ruin, rebellion,
and drink. So too, your lordship's reputation,
cheapened by the tarts and wastrels of Saint James's;
   there is not one of those weak-kneed
   bastards who—when drunk, dreaming
     of lost empires—will not
     bore me yet again

with that tale of how you outdanced all the braves
in the Seneca longhouse, so they might break
friendship with France, and further your British scheme
     to hold the Valley.
    And they tell it badly,
   beginning, like poor painters,
   with the atmosphere: smoky walls
of birch bark and ash staves, false faces hanging
in the murk with lips twisted and cheeks bulging
   as if they chewed a bitter root.
   Perhaps the tribal elders
     curse your high, frantic steps,
     or stare angrily

as, one by one, their young men rise and join you.
It is all so common. An artist would show
what moved you so: you wanted to be the fire
     kindled in their hall,
      you wanted not to cast
    shadows, but to be the source
    of all shadow, source of all light,

source of the very difference between them.
Decline, decline . . . The fire always less than God,
  and the dancer less than the fire,
  the shadow less than the man . . .
    And what of the shadow
    cast by the shadow?

Just how distant a relative would that be?
A young nephew, say, from Ireland, with his pack
full of pencils, brushes, signs of his longing
    for his own new world.
    It was yours already,
  the world I found; it required
  not artists, but artificers,
inheritors of established tracts, old deeds,
old visions, old vengeances, who pawn these off
  as their own. I, your mapmaker,
  recorded how your shadow fell
    on such and such a date,
    how it grew or shrank.

I'm at it still, a portraitist whose subject
escapes him, except in certain odd effects
caused by a shaky hand, or in mannerisms—
    defects in the style,
    a critic would call them—
  in which an old bitterness
  turns habitual elegance
against itself, turns light to half-light, darkness
to a shifting composition where nothing is clear
  except that you are present there
  and will never go away.
    You, who are the silent
    ground of all my speech . . .

Still, I must ask you this. Do you remember
how, when I first saw your country, I proposed
to paint its full extent, not in a series
    but as one great work?
    You laughed, and would not stop,
  except to say I must stay
  content with the place you set me—
my maps, my great house, your daughter in my bed,
a son's share of your estate—and not seek more.
  I knew then I must never hope
    that the Valley might be held
      in any hand but yours.
    Yes, and I know now

a son's portion is to starve, if he should fail
to consume his father, if he should not seize
the whole world for himself, and so learn to scorn
    all gifts but his own.
    I was too weak for that.
  I took what was offered,
    and I became the offering
the past demands. No one will remember me,
Uncle, unless they remember you as well.
  But will they recognize you,
    those who've not seen how I lived?
      I am your legacy.
      I am what is left.

Joseph Brant: Niagara, 1804

I have seen so much of Christian knavery and policy, that I am sick of Europe, which loves war and hates peace, therefore I want and long to have a wigwam near Great Pontiack.

Samuel Peters, LL.D., in a letter to the Mohawk chieftain
Joseph Brant, London, 1803

My Dear Samuel Peters,
I fear you do your continent and yourself
  some small disservice. Europe,
as your letter suggests, may hardly seem a true home
  to one whose birthplace (or birth-
  right, as you would have it) includes the wild shore
  of Memphramagog and those peaks

  along whose bleak chalk crests
Rogers fled after his raid on Saint Francis.
  (He told me some years later
that only the passing shadows of his rangers
  gave the boulders of White Face
  their famous appearance of a sinister
  watchfulness. Viewed just at twilight

  or noon, they were as blank
as a clean skull, and so filled his men with fear
  that as many were lost there
to madness as to the French and their Algonquin braves.)
  But perhaps your banishment
  is more a blessing than you have acknowledged?
  Birth assures a man of only

  one final rite, and homes
are always fatal to those poor voyagers
  whose inclination it is

    to return, who forget salvation lies in the hope
        that they need never come back.
    No world is fallen but in our sad efforts
        to recount it, as if the sum

        of broken trails, faint lines
    on parchment, could somehow equal your first sight
        of a long stretch of rapids,
a rocky shore, gray water at dawn as the haze lifts,
        or as a late mist settles,
    as memory settles when we come too near
        some original thing. Better,

    I think, never to speak
    of what we glimpse beyond ourselves, for fear
        we will lose everything
to windings that share nothing in common with this world.
        You ask how I liked London.
    I best recall the masked ball to which I came
        simply as myself, a Mohawk

    in full war dress: leggings,
    half my face painted, bearing a scalp axe, &ct.
        This caused such astonishment
(till then I had worn my well-cut crimson uniform,
        which is the prerogative
    of a British officer and gentleman)
        that the Turkish ambassador,

    who had mistaken me
    for some fop from Saint James's done up in plaster,
        dye, and gauze, twisted my nose
to see what lay beneath. I let out the same war cry
        that began the harsh battle

    at Oriskany, and as the dancing stopped,
      and the peers and the musicians

      sought refuge where they could,
    I raised my hatchet and leapt. The Turk's ladies
      fainted, he fled, and the ball
was judged a success. But later, in my room, I knelt—
      though this was not my custom—
    and prayed aloud, not for the King's great, failed cause,
      but for Sir William Johnson, Bart.,

      who was, as you must know,
    the first royal minister to my people,
      my brother-in-law, my friend,
yes, almost my father. What I had shown those good lords
      in jest—that one must either
    trust appearances or trust nothing at all—
      I had learned from him years before.

      You recall how the French
    and their Huron allies seized our northern forts
      one by one, the white ensigns
settling like fog over our forests, the ivory
      dress uniforms spilling down
    the St. Lawrence, as if even the dead rose
      against us and scattered the trails

      with hungry, wakeful bones.
    I was not yet sixteen. I still remember
      the horror of my first view
of a dead soldier's white leggings, white jacket, white face . . .
      a pale, empty face, nothing
    staring open-mouthed at nothing, at the world's
      foolscap wiped quite clean away.

I marched with Sir William
   and his company of Mohawks to relieve
      our last stronghold on Lake George,
which was not called by a king's name then, but by a saint's,
   a French saint's. How proud we were
   to rechristen it. How little the water
      changed, ready always to reflect

      any man's glance, a whore
   who, seeming to return our embraces, gave
      nothing that could not be had
by all comers, who forgot us as we turned away.
   But who can say if truly
   we knew ourselves there at all till that one glimpse,
      our features rippling, flickering,

made our blood lively with fear,
   with hatred, for the solitude waiting
      past her quicksilver surface.
Near Ticonderoga, we met a British platoon
   whose chief officer refused
   to join our advance, so great was his terror
      at the thought of a strange forest

   blooming with savages
   (those were his words) whose *murderous treachery*
      (or skillful native courage)
was the distorting echo of his own cowardice.
   Johnson beseeched him softly
   at first, but soon he knew the coward's nature
      beneath that imperious red

   husk of a uniform.
He did what great men do when the matter lies

very near the heart. He stood,
and in the same quiet tone he asked, "You will not come?"
    Then he untied one legging
    and threw it at the officer's feet. Each brave
        did likewise, and again Johnson's

    "You will not come?" again
    his Mohawks flung their leggings, again he spoke.
        Each time the English captain
refused, and grew more pale, like a lost hunter
    who stumbles into the rock den
    where the copperheads shed their skins. "You will not . . ."
        It was no longer a question.

    Johnson stood naked there
    with his men, raised his hatchet with theirs, his arms
        and body painted like theirs.
Once more: "You will not come." The officer fell backward,
    still shaking his head, trembling,
    and all the blades were thrown to the ground. All our just
        and civilized censure, all laws

    binding men in honor,
    had been invoked, had failed, and were now cast off,
        leaving the spirit revealed
in its pure rage. Dear Sir, can you wonder if I thought
    Sir William a great prophet
    after that night. He showed me the prime mover,
        first cause of all the civilities

    and gestures of mankind,
    of the world we make for ourselves: a hatred
        for what would slip from our hands,
the cowardly, shimmering fabric of foreign things.

If we love appearances,
   it is because this anger finds its best home
      in opposites—courtly manners,

   peaceful towns, ripe orchards—
      so immanent is it in every detail
         of our lives. He taught me trust,
piety, and devotion, and what I saw unveiled
      in him, I took for gospel.
   As I had taken his Christian god for mine,
      I now saw this acrid spirit

      reflected everywhere:
   traced in firelight on a friend's face, on my face
      shining in a sharpened knife . . .
or in those features I thought were mine. I knew myself
      no longer. I was possessed
   by the desire to carve the world's forms away,
      to know this demon more purely,

      to hoard all his power.
   So my life went on, a litany of death
      repeated over, over,
leading nowhere. Or should I say it led me always,
      like a trail of ill omens—
   blank skull of a wolf, footprints circling your own—
      nearer to what I most regret:

      dawn at Cherry Valley,
   Butler smiling, unsheathing his sword, crying
      "Let my bloody angels play!"
There is no need to recount that slaughter, to place blame,
      or to lead you, my patient
   friend, much further through those horrors that changed me
      from acolyte to a mere man.

I found no vision there,
   only human shards, only an empty lane
      where a dead man's outstretched hand
pointed toward a building as yet untouched by flame,
      except for one stain of soot
   on the oak door, a dark trace, like a profile . . .
      Sir William's, I thought, or my own.

   If I was startled then,
      it was nothing to what followed. Within the house,
         someone sang, a low voice,
almost like that of a stream, its sweet, unending song.
      In the parlor, a woman
   sat spinning, and when she looked at me I saw
      neither fear nor astonishment.

   She went on with her work,
      and although I begged her urgently to flee,
         to hide, or else to prepare
for death, she continued to sing. When I fell silent,
      she wound the thread once again,
   and said there was no danger, that Joseph Brant
      was leader of the raiders

         and a great friend of hers,
      and he would surely come to find her. Dear Sir
         I was streaked with paint and blood
so that Johnson himself would not have known me, but still
      her lack of recognition
   so unnerved me that I was doubtful even
      of my own being, or of hers.

   I did not know her name.
      Yet as her twisted thread reeled out, as her hands
         shone and vanished through the wheel

and she sang again, I knew that I stood near the hub
    of all things, alone with a force
  far beyond either my hatred or my awe,
    an outpouring so endlessly

    patient as to seem still,
  a pattern running through my life, a pattern
    which was all of life, changed now
as my vision wove it in her image. This was home:
    not the heart of the world, but
  the world itself, emptied of desire, waiting
    for me to create it anew,

    to wind its stiff fibers
  and feel my own strand passed around the spindle.
    So our homes find us, my friend,
when our spirits dwindle, when our shadows no longer
    quicken the earth's reticence.
  If you are that tired, you have earned your passage.
    There will be no need to seek it.

Your servant,

Joseph Brant

Notes

Part One. A Lesson from the Hudson River School

LITTLE SUITE FOR EDVARD MUNCH.

The sixth and seventh lines of the first section are adapted from a statement of Munch's, quoted in Frederick B. Deknatel's *Edvard Munch* (New York: Chanticleer Press, 1950).

FOR THE ORTHODOX.

The first line of the second section and the final two lines of the third section are closely adapted from lines in Tsvetayeva's "Praise to the Rich" and "Poems for Blok," respectively (*Marina Tsvetayeva: Selected Poems*, translated by Elaine Feinstein, London: Oxford University Press, 1971).

MOUNT HOPE: TO WELDON KEES.

The italicized phrases are from Kees's poem "The City as Hero" (*The Collected Poems of Weldon Kees*, edited by Donald Justice, Lincoln: University of Nebraska Press, 1975).

Part Two. A Mirror for Loyalists

Several volumes provided valuable accounts of the characters and events on which the poems in this section are based: the two editions of James Thomas Flexner's biography of Sir William Johnson, *Mohawk Baronet* (New York: Harper & Brothers, 1959) and *Lord of the Mohawks* (Boston: Little, Brown, 1979); Barbara Graymont's *The Iroquois in the American Revolution* (Syracuse: Syracuse University Press, 1972), which was especially helpful in clarifying the circumstances surrounding the raid on Cherry Valley; and William L. Stone's *Life of Joseph Brant—Thayendanegea* (New York: George Dearborn and Co., 1838). The letter to Colonel Alden may be found in Graymont's history; the original version of the speech attributed to William of Canajoharie is quoted by both Flexner and Graymont; the letter to Joseph Brant from Samuel Peters may be found in Stone's *Life*. Departures from historical fact and scholarly interpretation are my own.

GUY JOHNSON: LONDON, 1788.
The epigraph is taken from *The Works of William Hogarth; in a Series of Engravings: with Descriptions and a Comment on Their Moral Tendency*, by the Rev. John Trusler. *To which are added Anecdotes of the Author and his Works*, by J. Hogarth and J. Nichols (London: Jones and Co., 1833).

Library of Congress Cataloging in Publication Data

Smith, Jordan, 1954-
   An apology for loving the old hymns.

   (Princeton series of contemporary poets)
   Includes bibliographical and references.
   I. Title.   II. Series.
PS3569.M5375515A88   811'.54   82-47615
ISBN 0-691-06530-6   AACR2
ISBN 0-691-01399-3 (pbk.)

GPSR Authorized Representative: Easy Access System Europe - Mustamäe tee 50, 10621 Tallinn, Estonia, gpsr.requests@easproject.com

www.ingramcontent.com/pod-product-compliance
Lightning Source LLC
Chambersburg PA
CBHW081422230426
43668CB00016B/2327